This playbook belongs to:

_____

Dear Visionaries and Creatives,

I'm super excited to take this journey with you as we strategize a winning plan every Monday of this year! My friends, you will no longer have to dread "When *Monday* Comes". This playbook will assist you in winning championships! There are countless plays in this journal that will help you navigate your creativity and execute on a higher level!

Consider every Monday to be a new week, a clean slate to begin again, and a fresh start to finish what you have started! Winning is in your DNA, so clothe yourself with STRENGTH and adorn your face with a SMILE. You have what it takes to build something extraordinary! Remember, you are Heaven's expression in the Earth. In forming a partnership with Mondays, you will be able to blaze a trail every week! The best plan is a written one, so let's get it out of your head and into your hands. A wise man once told me "work in silence and let success be your noise"! Enough talking, let's get to work!!!

Sincerely your coach,

Dr. Stephanie Jennings

Who are you and what do you want to become?

What is your legacy?

What is your purpose?

Word of The Year!

The vision for your life creates the **DISCIPLINE** for your life.
—unknown

Who is God to You?

- El Shaddai (Lord God Almighty)
- El Elyon (The Most High God)
- Adonai (Lord, Master)
- Yahweh (Lord, Jehovah)
- Jehovah Nissi (The Lord My Banner)
- Jehovah Raah (The Lord My Shepherd)
- Jehovah Rapha (The Lord That Heals)
- Jehovah Shammah (The Lord Is There)
- Jehovah Tsidkenu (The Lord Our Righteousness)
- Jehovah Mekoddishkem (The Lord Who Sanctifies You)
- El Olam (The Everlasting God)
- Jehovah Gmolah (The Lord Our Recompense)
- Jehovah Jireh (The Lord Will Provide)
- Jehovah Shalom (The Lord Is Peace)
- Jehovah Sabaoth (The Lord of Hosts)

Daily Affirmations

I can do All things through Christ that gives me strength (Phil 4:13)

Today my hands will go to work to yield the increase that belongs to me

Wealth and riches shall be me in my house, because I can do All things through Christ that gives me strength

I Am a money magnetic and money comes to me easily and frequently

My potential is the answer to someone's cry, so now I walk in the plans, purposes and promises of God

I am an innovator with a reformers anointing infiltrating the seven mountains of influence: Arts & Entertainment, Business, Media, Church, Family, Education, and Government

DEAR Monday

Personal Growth

Letter to your *future* self

DATE: _____

"The me you see is not the me that will be."
-Dr. Stephanie Jennings

Strengthening Your Core

You can not conquer what you're not willing to confront. Begin to strengthen your weaknesses and build on your strengths.

Strengths	Weakness

Ask 3 people to see if they can confirm your strengths and weaknesses

Notes

7 Mountains of Influence

These are the **7** systems that INFLUENCE the WORLD and SHAPE our CULTURE:

1. EDUCATION
2. FAMILY
3. RELIGION (Church)
4. GOVERNMENT
5. ARTS and ENTERTAINMENT
6. BUSINESS (Economy)
7. MEDIA

Below are questions that will help you level up and pivot in business and daily living:

What is your mountain of influence?

_____
_____
_____
_____

What is your calling / assignment?

_____
_____
_____
_____

What is your mandate?

_____
_____
_____
_____

What are your Core Values and Beliefs?

_____
_____
_____
_____

What does winning look like for you?

_____
_____
_____
_____

What is undermining your WIN?

_____
_____
_____
_____

Who will benefit from your WIN?

_____
_____
_____
_____

What will you do after your WIN?

_____
_____
_____
_____

Philippians 4:6 AMPC
Do not fret or have any anxiety about anything, but in every circumstance and in everything, by prayer and petition (definite requests), with thanksgiving, continue to make your wants known to God.

Prayer Targets

1 John 5:14-15 NKJV

14 Now this is the confidence that we have in Him, that if we ask anything according to His will, He hears us. 15 And if we know that He hears us, whatever we ask, we know that we have the petitions that we have asked of Him.

> What scripture or prophetic word from God will you meditate on?

Joshua 1:8 (KJV)

This book of the law shall not depart out of thy mouth; but thou shalt meditate therein day and night, that thou mayest observe to do according to all that is written therein: for then thou shalt make thy way prosperous, and then thou shalt have good success.

DEAR Monday

Prophetic Pursuits

Vision Board

YEAR: _____

"I think that the greatest gift God ever gave man is not the gift of sight but the gift of vision. Sight is a function of the eyes, but vision is a function of the heart."

—Myles Munroe

"The more that you read, the more things you will know. The more that you learn, the more places you'll go."
— Dr. Seuss

TITLE	GENRE	DATE

Financial Goals

YEARLY: _____

MONTHLY: _____

WEEKLY: _____

Desired Credit Score

3 mos:

6 mos:

12 mos:

Remember!

Set savings goals and document your progress!!

Notes

What you do in your day will determine your pay!

—Dr. Stephanie Jennings

Goal:

Start Date:

Deadline:

Date	Amount

Total: _____

DREAM

Divine Revealed Events Awaiting Manifestation

Write your dreams and color in the cloud when they manifest

"All our **dreams** can come true, if we have the courage to pursue them."

~Walt Disney

DEAR Monday

Productivity

Identifying Time Robbers

Eph 5:15-16 (AMPC)

15 Look carefully then how you walk! Live purposefully and worthily and accurately, not as the unwise and witless, but as wise (sensible, intelligent people), 16 Making the very most of the time [buying up each opportunity], because the days are evil.

(people and things stealing your time)

1.
2.
3.
4.
5.

> You will never become a 7 figure earner doing minimum wage jobs!
>
> —Dr. Stephanie Jennings

Identifying Time Tellers

Eph 5:15-16 (AMPC)

15 Look carefully then how you walk! Live purposefully and worthily and accurately, not as the unwise and witless, but as wise (sensible, intelligent people), 16 Making the very most of the time [buying up each opportunity], because the days are evil.

(people and things annointed to remind you of the time that you're in)

1.
2.
3.
4.
5.

> You will never become a 7 figure earner doing minimum wage jobs!
>
> -Dr. Stephanie Jennings

Morning Routine

In order to be sucessful you must have to have a routine.

QUARTER 1

TIME	ACTIVITY
:	
:	
:	
:	
:	
:	

QUARTER 2

TIME	ACTIVITY
:	
:	
:	
:	
:	
:	

QUARTER 3

TIME	ACTIVITY
:	
:	
:	
:	
:	
:	

QUARTER 4

TIME	ACTIVITY
:	
:	
:	
:	
:	
:	

Night Routine

In order to be successful you must have a routine.

"The secret of your future is hidden in your daily routine."
—Mike Murdock

QUARTER 1

TIME	ACTIVITY
:	
:	
:	
:	
:	
:	

QUARTER 2

TIME	ACTIVITY
:	
:	
:	
:	
:	
:	

QUARTER 3

TIME	ACTIVITY
:	
:	
:	
:	
:	
:	

QUARTER 4

TIME	ACTIVITY
:	
:	
:	
:	
:	
:	

Creating New Habits

New Habits	Mon	Tue	Wed	Thu	Fri	Sat	Sun
_____							
_____							
_____							
_____							
_____							
_____							
_____							
_____							
_____							
_____							
_____							
_____							
_____							

"If you are going to achieve excellence in big things, you develop the habit in little matters. Excellence is not an exception, it is a prevailing attitude".
— Colin Powell

Motivation

DEAR Monday

Planning

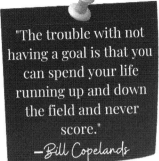

"The trouble with not having a goal is that you can spend your life running up and down the field and never score."
—Bill Copelands

- [ ] _____
- [ ] _____
- [ ] _____
- [ ] _____
- [ ] _____
- [ ] _____
- [ ] _____
- [ ] _____
- [ ] _____
- [ ] _____
- [ ] _____
- [ ] _____
- [ ] _____
- [ ] _____

1st Quarter Wins!

Pick one of your goals and map it out. "Everything is paid for with a thought."

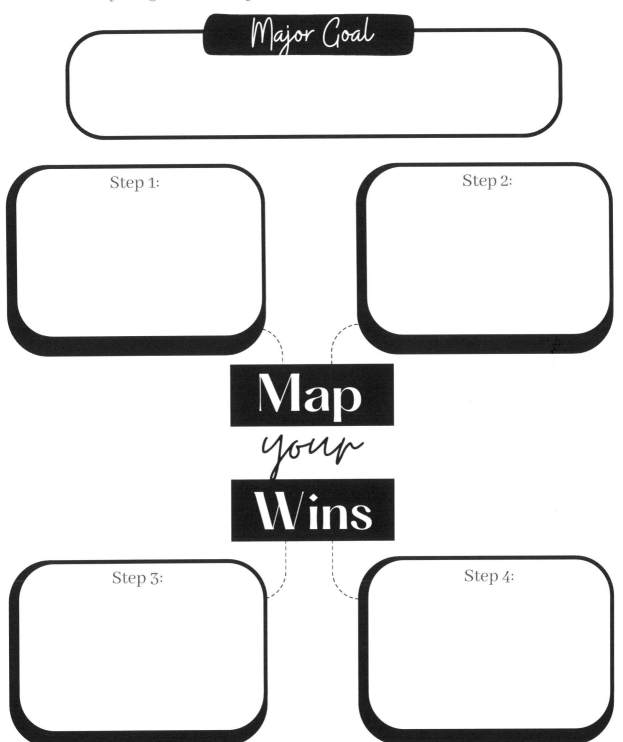

2nd Quarter Wins!

Pick one of your goals and map it out. "Everything is paid for with a thought."

3rd Quarter Wins!

Pick one of your goals and map it out. "Everything is paid for with a thought."

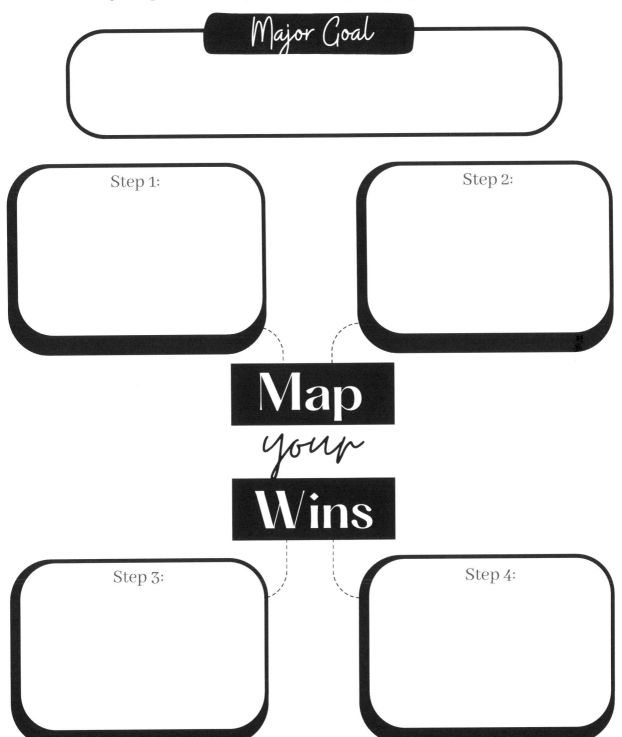

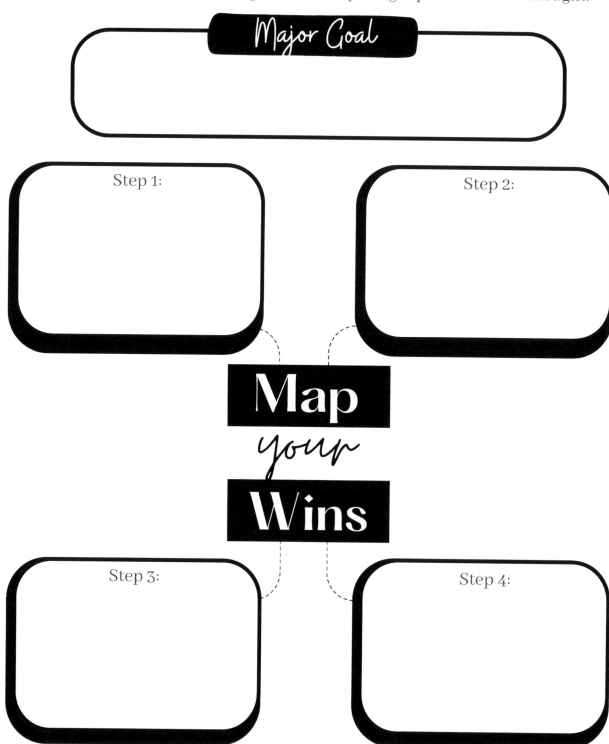

Month: _____

EVERY DAY IS A FRESH START

Mon	Tue	Wed	Thurs	Fri	Sat	Sun
Wake Up & WIN!						

"Motivation gets you going, but discipline keeps you growing"

-John C. Maxwell

Month: _____

EVERY DAY IS A FRESH START

Mon	Tue	Wed	Thurs	Fri	Sat	Sun
Wake Up & WIN!						

"Motivation gets you going, but discipline keeps you growing"

–John C. Maxwell

Month: _____

Mon	Tue	Wed	Thurs	Fri	Sat	Sun
Wake Up & WIN!						

> "Motivation gets you going, but discipline keeps you growing."
> — John C. Maxwell

Month: _____

EVERY DAY IS A FRESH START

Mon	Tue	Wed	Thurs	Fri	Sat	Sun
Wake Up & WIN!						

"Motivation gets you going, but discipline keeps you growing."

—John C. Maxwell

Month: _____

Mon	Tue	Wed	Thurs	Fri	Sat	Sun
Wake Up & WIN!						

"Motivation gets you going, but discipline keeps you growing"

—John C. Maxwell

Month: _____

EVERY DAY IS A FRESH START

Mon	Tue	Wed	Thurs	Fri	Sat	Sun
Wake Up & WIN!						

"Motivation gets you going, but discipline keeps you growing"

—John C. Maxwell

Month: _____

Mon	Tue	Wed	Thurs	Fri	Sat	Sun
Wake Up & WIN!						

"Motivation gets you going, but discipline keeps you growing"

—John C. Maxwell

Month: _____

EVERY DAY IS A FRESH START

Mon	Tue	Wed	Thurs	Fri	Sat	Sun
Wake Up & WIN!						

"Motivation gets you going, but discipline keeps you growing"

-John C. Maxwell

Month: _____

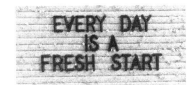

Mon	Tue	Wed	Thurs	Fri	Sat	Sun
Wake Up & WIN!						

"Motivation gets you going, but discipline keeps you growing"
— John C. Maxwell

Month: _____

EVERY DAY IS A FRESH START

Mon	Tue	Wed	Thurs	Fri	Sat	Sun
Wake Up & WIN!						

"Motivation gets you going, but discipline keeps you <u>growing</u>"

−John C. Maxwell

Month: _____

Mon	Tue	Wed	Thurs	Fri	Sat	Sun
Wake Up & WIN!						

"Motivation gets you going, but discipline keeps you growing"

—John C. Maxwell

Month: _____

EVERY DAY IS A FRESH START

Mon	Tue	Wed	Thurs	Fri	Sat	Sun
Wake Up & WIN!						

"Motivation gets you going, but discipline keeps you growing"

—John C. Maxwell

I decree and declare *extreme* focus, consistent faith and <u>fresh ideas</u> daily.

"Small disciplines repeated with consistency every day lead to great achievements gained slowly over time."

— John C Maxwell

Things to Accomplish

- _____
- _____
- _____
- _____
- _____
- _____
- _____

Action List

- _____
- _____
- _____
- _____
- _____
- _____
- _____

For Tomorrow

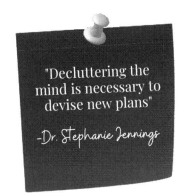

IDEAS

THOUGHTS

REMEMBER ME

DUMP IT

Notes

DEAR *Monday*

I decree and declare the full *shalom* of God is upon my life nothing broken and nothing missing.

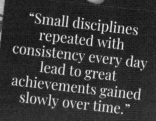

"Small disciplines repeated with consistency every day lead to great achievements gained slowly over time."

— John C Maxwell

Things to Accomplish

- _____
- _____
- _____
- _____
- _____
- _____
- _____

Action List

- _____
- _____
- _____
- _____
- _____
- _____
- _____

For Tomorrow

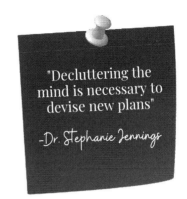

IDEAS

THOUGHTS

REMEMBER ME

DUMP IT

Notes

DEAR *Monday*

I decree and declare that I will operate from the *miracle* realm.

Things to Accomplish

-
-
-
-
-
-
-

Action List

-
-
-
-
-
-
-

"Decluttering the mind is necessary to devise new plans"

-Dr. Stephanie Jennings

IDEAS

THOUGHTS

REMEMBER ME

DUMP IT

Notes

I decree and declare that I am taking <u>flight</u> and flowing in God's will.

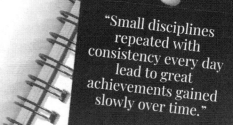

Things to Accomplish

- _____
- _____
- _____
- _____
- _____
- _____
- _____

Action List

- _____
- _____
- _____
- _____
- _____
- _____
- _____
- _____

For Tomorrow

"Decluttering the mind is necessary to devise new plans"

-Dr. Stephanie Jennings

IDEAS

THOUGHTS

REMEMBER ME

DUMP IT

Notes

I *decree* and declare that every God idea will yield great wealth and riches.

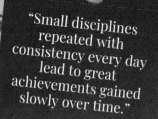

"Small disciplines repeated with consistency every day lead to great achievements gained slowly over time."

– John C Maxwell

Things to Accomplish

- _____
- _____
- _____
- _____
- _____
- _____
- _____

Action List

- _____
- _____
- _____
- _____
- _____
- _____
- _____

For Tomorrow

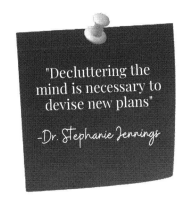

"Decluttering the mind is necessary to devise new plans"

-Dr. Stephanie Jennings

IDEAS

THOUGHTS

REMEMBER ME

DUMP IT

Notes

DEAR Monday

I decree and declare
my hands will
produce millions.

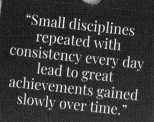

"Small disciplines repeated with consistency every day lead to great achievements gained slowly over time."

– John C Maxwell

Things to Accomplish

- _____
- _____
- _____
- _____
- _____
- _____
- _____

Action List

- _____
- _____
- _____
- _____
- _____
- _____
- _____

For Tomorrow

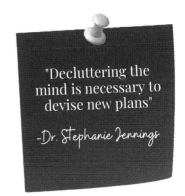

IDEAS

THOUGHTS

REMEMBER ME

DUMP IT

Notes

DEAR Monday

I decree and declare *prophetic* strategies and *apostolic* flow.

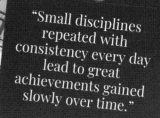

"Small disciplines repeated with consistency every day lead to great achievements gained slowly over time."

— John C Maxwell

Things to Accomplish

-
-
-
-
-
-
-

Action List

-
-
-
-
-
-
-

For Tomorrow

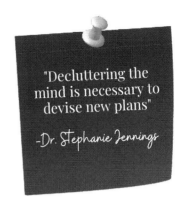

"Decluttering the mind is necessary to devise new plans"
-Dr. Stephanie Jennings

IDEAS

THOUGHTS

REMEMBER ME

DUMP IT

Notes

DEAR Monday

I decree and declare that I have *favor* with God and man.

"Small disciplines repeated with consistency every day lead to great achievements gained slowly over time."

- John C Maxwell

Things to Accomplish

-
-
-
-
-
-
-

Action List

-
-
-
-
-
-
-

For Tomorrow

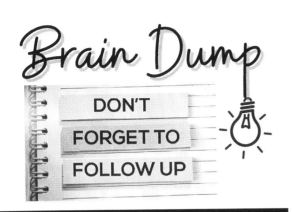
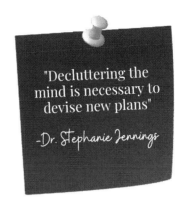

IDEAS

THOUGHTS

REMEMBER ME

DUMP IT

Notes

DEAR Monday

I decree and declare that I *operate* from the King's wealth.

"Small disciplines repeated with consistency every day lead to great achievements gained slowly over time."

— John C Maxwell

Things to Accomplish

- _____
- _____
- _____
- _____
- _____
- _____
- _____

Action List

- _____
- _____
- _____
- _____
- _____
- _____
- _____

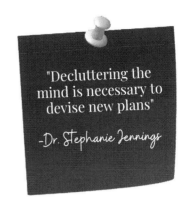

IDEAS

THOUGHTS

REMEMBER ME

DUMP IT

Notes

DEAR Monday

I decree and declare that all project budgets are met and I will <u>operate</u> from the place of *overflow*.

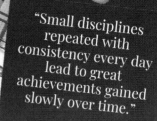

"Small disciplines repeated with consistency every day lead to great achievements gained slowly over time."

– John C. Maxwell

Things to Accomplish

- _____
- _____
- _____
- _____
- _____
- _____
- _____

Action List

- _____
- _____
- _____
- _____
- _____
- _____
- _____

For Tomorrow 💡

IDEAS

THOUGHTS

REMEMBER ME

DUMP IT

Notes

I decree and declare my steps are *ordered* and <u>success</u> is my outcome.

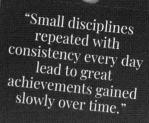

"Small disciplines repeated with consistency every day lead to great achievements gained slowly over time."

— John C Maxwell

Things to Accomplish

-
-
-
-
-
-
-

Action List

-
-
-
-
-
-
-

For Tomorrow

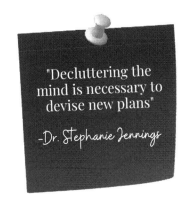

IDEAS

THOUGHTS

REMEMBER ME

DUMP IT

Notes

DEAR Monday

I decree and declare my products and services are in *high* demand.

Things to Accomplish

- _____
- _____
- _____
- _____
- _____
- _____
- _____

Action List

- _____
- _____
- _____
- _____
- _____
- _____
- _____

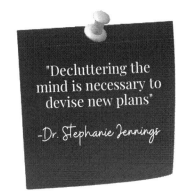

IDEAS

THOUGHTS

REMEMBER ME

DUMP IT

Notes

DEAR Monday

I decree and declare that my *investments* will yield great dividends.

"Small disciplines repeated with consistency every day lead to great achievements gained slowly over time."

– John C Maxwell

Things to Accomplish

- _____
- _____
- _____
- _____
- _____
- _____
- _____

Action List

- _____
- _____
- _____
- _____
- _____
- _____
- _____

For Tomorrow

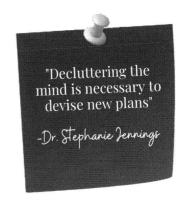

IDEAS

THOUGHTS

REMEMBER ME

DUMP IT

Notes

I decree and declare passive and aggressive *income* in my financial portfolio.

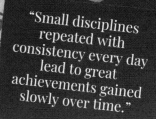

"Small disciplines repeated with consistency every day lead to great achievements gained slowly over time."

— John C Maxwell

Things to Accomplish

- _____
- _____
- _____
- _____
- _____
- _____
- _____

Action List

- _____
- _____
- _____
- _____
- _____
- _____
- _____

For Tomorrow

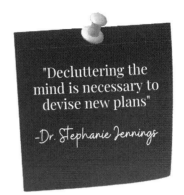

IDEAS

THOUGHTS

REMEMBER ME

DUMP IT

Notes

DEAR Monday

I decree and declare that my team will flow in the spirit of unity and we will *operate* from the place of the commanded blessings.

"Small disciplines repeated with consistency every day lead to great achievements gained slowly over time."

— John C Maxwell

Things to Accomplish

- ___
- ___
- ___
- ___
- ___
- ___
- ___

Action List

- ___
- ___
- ___
- ___
- ___
- ___
- ___

For Tomorrow

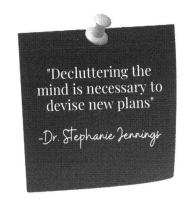

"Decluttering the mind is necessary to devise new plans"

-Dr. Stephanie Jennings

IDEAS

THOUGHTS

REMEMBER ME

DUMP IT

Notes

DEAR *Monday*

I decree and declare my team *moves* in <u>agility</u> and <u>accuracy</u> with every assignment.

"Small disciplines repeated with consistency every day lead to great achievements gained slowly over time."

– John C Maxwell

Things to Accomplish

- _____
- _____
- _____
- _____
- _____
- _____
- _____

Action List

- _____
- _____
- _____
- _____
- _____
- _____
- _____

For Tomorrow 💡

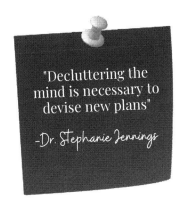

IDEAS

THOUGHTS

REMEMBER ME

DUMP IT

Notes

DEAR Monday

I decree and declare new doors and new *opportunities* will <u>find</u> my company.

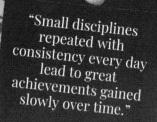

"Small disciplines repeated with consistency every day lead to great achievements gained slowly over time."

— John C Maxwell

Things to Accomplish

- _____
- _____
- _____
- _____
- _____
- _____
- _____

Action List

- _____
- _____
- _____
- _____
- _____
- _____
- _____

For Tomorrow

"Decluttering the mind is necessary to devise new plans"

-Dr. Stephanie Jennings

IDEAS

THOUGHTS

REMEMBER ME

DUMP IT

Notes

I *decree* and declare that the ~~spirit of greed~~ and ~~godlessness~~ is a nonfactor in my life.

"Small disciplines repeated with consistency every day lead to great achievements gained slowly over time."

– John C Maxwell

Things to Accomplish

-
-
-
-
-
-
-

Action List

-
-
-
-
-
-
-

For Tomorrow

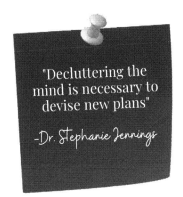

"Decluttering the mind is necessary to devise new plans"

-Dr. Stephanie Jennings

IDEAS

THOUGHTS

REMEMBER ME

DUMP IT

Notes

I decree and declare I operate from the *treasures* of heaven.

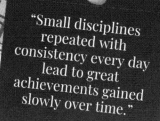

"Small disciplines repeated with consistency every day lead to great achievements gained slowly over time."

— John C. Maxwell

Things to Accomplish

-
-
-
-
-
-
-

Action List

-
-
-
-
-
-
-

"Decluttering the mind is necessary to devise new plans"
—Dr. Stephanie Jennings

IDEAS

THOUGHTS

REMEMBER ME

DUMP IT

Notes

I decree and declare the earth will yield the *harvest* that belongs to me.

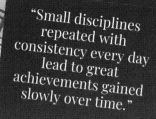

"Small disciplines repeated with consistency every day lead to great achievements gained slowly over time."

– John C Maxwell

Things to Accomplish

-
-
-
-
-
-
-

Action List

-
-
-
-
-
-
-

For Tomorrow

"Decluttering the mind is necessary to devise new plans"

-Dr. Stephanie Jennings

IDEAS

THOUGHTS

REMEMBER ME

DUMP IT

Notes

I decree and declare
that I *win* twelve months
out of the year.

"Small disciplines repeated with consistency every day lead to great achievements gained slowly over time."

— John C Maxwell

Things to Accomplish

-
-
-
-
-
-
-

Action List

-
-
-
-
-
-
-

For Tomorrow

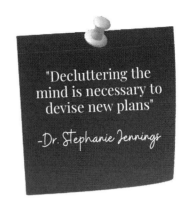

IDEAS

THOUGHTS

REMEMBER ME

DUMP IT

Notes

DEAR *Monday*

I decree and declare that this will be a week of <u>great wins</u> and great *accomplishments*.

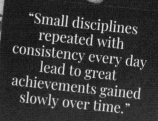

"Small disciplines repeated with consistency every day lead to great achievements gained slowly over time."

— John C. Maxwell

Things to Accomplish

- _____
- _____
- _____
- _____
- _____
- _____
- _____

Action List

- _____
- _____
- _____
- _____
- _____
- _____
- _____

For Tomorrow

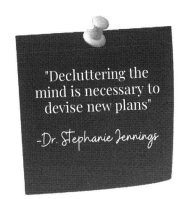

"Decluttering the mind is necessary to devise new plans"
-Dr. Stephanie Jennings

IDEAS

THOUGHTS

REMEMBER ME

DUMP IT

Notes

DEAR *Monday*

I decree and declare extreme *execution* and great endurance.

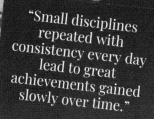

"Small disciplines repeated with consistency every day lead to great achievements gained slowly over time."

— John C Maxwell

Things to Accomplish

- _____
- _____
- _____
- _____
- _____
- _____
- _____

Action List

- _____
- _____
- _____
- _____
- _____
- _____
- _____

For Tomorrow

"Decluttering the mind is necessary to devise new plans"

-Dr. Stephanie Jennings

IDEAS

THOUGHTS

REMEMBER ME

DUMP IT

Notes

DEAR Monday

I decree and declare that investments and inventories will *sell* out

"Small disciplines repeated with consistency every day lead to great achievements gained slowly over time."

— John C Maxwell

Things to Accomplish

-
-
-
-
-
-
-

Action List

-
-
-
-
-
-
-

For Tomorrow 💡

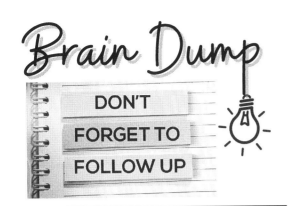

Brain Dump

DON'T FORGET TO FOLLOW UP

"Decluttering the mind is necessary to devise new plans"

—Dr. Stephanie Jennings

IDEAS

THOUGHTS

REMEMBER ME

DUMP IT

Notes

I decree and declare WINS on *top* of WINS.

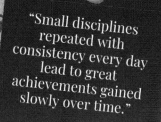

"Small disciplines repeated with consistency every day lead to great achievements gained slowly over time."

— John C Maxwell

Things to Accomplish

- _____
- _____
- _____
- _____
- _____
- _____
- _____

Action List

- _____
- _____
- _____
- _____
- _____
- _____
- _____

IDEAS

THOUGHTS

REMEMBER ME

DUMP IT

Notes

DEAR Monday

I decree and declare your _assignment_ in the <u>earth</u> will be accelerated.

"Small disciplines repeated with consistency every day lead to great achievements gained slowly over time."

— John C Maxwell

Things to Accomplish

- _____
- _____
- _____
- _____
- _____
- _____
- _____

Action List

- _____
- _____
- _____
- _____
- _____
- _____
- _____

For Tomorrow 💡

IDEAS

THOUGHTS

REMEMBER ME

DUMP IT

Notes

DEAR *Monday*

I decree and declare your *purpose* will produce great things in the earth and heal many people.

"Small disciplines repeated with consistency every day lead to great achievements gained slowly over time."

— John C Maxwell

Things to Accomplish

- _____
- _____
- _____
- _____
- _____
- _____
- _____

Action List

- _____
- _____
- _____
- _____
- _____
- _____
- _____

For Tomorrow

IDEAS

THOUGHTS

REMEMBER ME

DUMP IT

Notes

I decree and declare *restoration* from <u>anything</u> that has been stolen from the enemy.

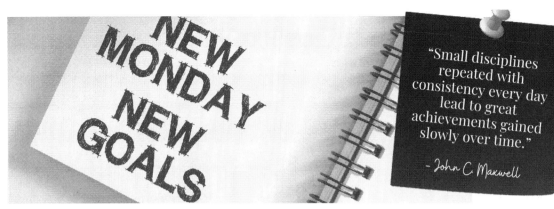

"Small disciplines repeated with consistency every day lead to great achievements gained slowly over time."

– John C Maxwell

Things to Accomplish

- _____
- _____
- _____
- _____
- _____
- _____
- _____

Action List

- _____
- _____
- _____
- _____
- _____
- _____
- _____

For Tomorrow

IDEAS

THOUGHTS

REMEMBER ME

DUMP IT

Notes

I decree and declare divine *connections* and <u>divine</u> directions.

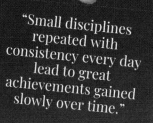

"Small disciplines repeated with consistency every day lead to great achievements gained slowly over time."

– John C Maxwell

Things to Accomplish

- _____
- _____
- _____
- _____
- _____
- _____
- _____

Action List

- _____
- _____
- _____
- _____
- _____
- _____
- _____

For Tomorrow

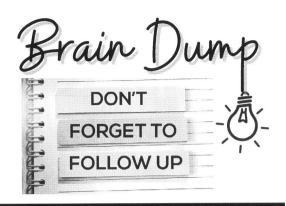 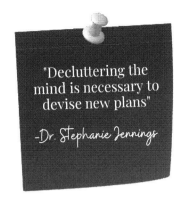

IDEAS

THOUGHTS

REMEMBER ME

DUMP IT

Notes

DEAR Monday

I decree and declare *freedom* and the <u>full shalom</u> of God.

"Small disciplines repeated with consistency every day lead to great achievements gained slowly over time."

— John C Maxwell

Things to Accomplish

-
-
-
-
-
-
-

Action List

-
-
-
-
-
-
-

For Tomorrow

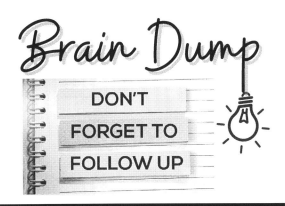
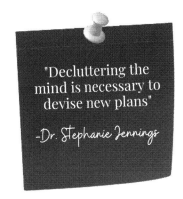

IDEAS

THOUGHTS

REMEMBER ME

DUMP IT

Notes

I decree and declare new territories and *triumphant* victories.

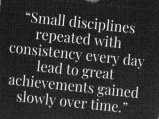

"Small disciplines repeated with consistency every day lead to great achievements gained slowly over time."

– John C Maxwell

Things to Accomplish

- _____
- _____
- _____
- _____
- _____
- _____
- _____

Action List

- _____
- _____
- _____
- _____
- _____
- _____
- _____

For Tomorrow

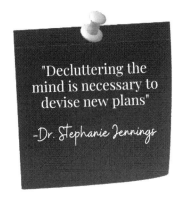

IDEAS

THOUGHTS

REMEMBER ME

DUMP IT

Notes

I decree and declare peace, *power*, and prosperity will be my portion.

> "Small disciplines repeated with consistency every day lead to great achievements gained slowly over time."
>
> – John C Maxwell

Things to Accomplish

- _____
- _____
- _____
- _____
- _____
- _____
- _____

Action List

- _____
- _____
- _____
- _____
- _____
- _____
- _____

For Tomorrow

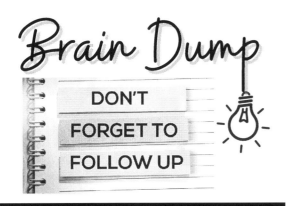
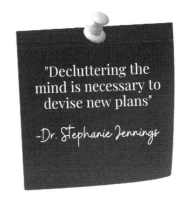

IDEAS

THOUGHTS

REMEMBER ME

DUMP IT

Notes

DEAR Monday

I decree and declare the demonstration of *power* and might in Jesus name.

"Small disciplines repeated with consistency every day lead to great achievements gained slowly over time."

– John C Maxwell

Things to Accomplish

- _____
- _____
- _____
- _____
- _____
- _____
- _____

Action List

- _____
- _____
- _____
- _____
- _____
- _____
- _____

For Tomorrow

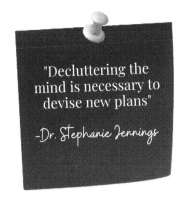

IDEAS

THOUGHTS

REMEMBER ME

DUMP IT

Notes

I decree and declare manifested *promises*.

"Small disciplines repeated with consistency every day lead to great achievements gained slowly over time."

– John C. Maxwell

Things to Accomplish

- _____
- _____
- _____
- _____
- _____
- _____
- _____

Action List

- _____
- _____
- _____
- _____
- _____
- _____
- _____

For Tomorrow

IDEAS

THOUGHTS

REMEMBER ME

DUMP IT

Notes

DEAR *Monday*

I decree and declare new doors, new <u>fortunes</u>, new *strengths*, new <u>victories</u>, and new <u>momentum</u>.

"Small disciplines repeated with consistency every day lead to great achievements gained slowly over time."

– John C Maxwell

Things to Accomplish

- _____
- _____
- _____
- _____
- _____
- _____
- _____

Action List

- _____
- _____
- _____
- _____
- _____
- _____
- _____

For Tomorrow

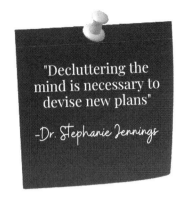

IDEAS

THOUGHTS

REMEMBER ME

DUMP IT

Notes

DEAR Monday

I decree and declare a week of *exceeding* <u>abundance</u> and more than I can ask or think.

"Small disciplines repeated with consistency every day lead to great achievements gained slowly over time."

– John C Maxwell

Things to Accomplish

- _____
- _____
- _____
- _____
- _____
- _____
- _____

Action List

- _____
- _____
- _____
- _____
- _____
- _____
- _____

For Tomorrow

IDEAS

THOUGHTS

REMEMBER ME

DUMP IT

Notes

DEAR Monday

I decree and declare I will trust God's <u>word</u> and <u>rest</u> in His promises.

"Small disciplines repeated with consistency every day lead to great achievements gained slowly over time."

– John C Maxwell

Things to Accomplish

-
-
-
-
-
-
-

Action List

-
-
-
-
-
-
-

For Tomorrow

IDEAS

THOUGHTS

REMEMBER ME

DUMP IT

Notes

I decree and declare I will operate in *divine* wisdom, wealth, and knowledge.

"Small disciplines repeated with consistency every day lead to great achievements gained slowly over time."

– John C Maxwell

Things to Accomplish

-
-
-
-
-
-
-

Action List

-
-
-
-
-
-
-

For Tomorrow

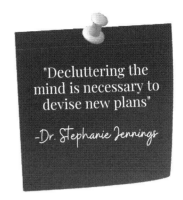

IDEAS

THOUGHTS

REMEMBER ME

DUMP IT

Notes

DEAR *Monday*

I decree and declare a *lifting* of my finances, fortunes, and *future*.

"Small disciplines repeated with consistency every day lead to great achievements gained slowly over time."

– John C Maxwell

Things to Accomplish

- _____
- _____
- _____
- _____
- _____
- _____
- _____

Action List

- _____
- _____
- _____
- _____
- _____
- _____
- _____

For Tomorrow 💡

IDEAS

THOUGHTS

REMEMBER ME

DUMP IT

Notes

I decree and declare my brain will function at *maximum* level and my mind will process <u>new ideas</u>.

"Small disciplines repeated with consistency every day lead to great achievements gained slowly over time."

– John C Maxwell

Things to Accomplish

- _____
- _____
- _____
- _____
- _____
- _____
- _____

Action List

- _____
- _____
- _____
- _____
- _____
- _____
- _____

For Tomorrow

IDEAS

THOUGHTS

REMEMBER ME

DUMP IT

Notes

I decree and declare a new flow, new moves, and new *wealth*.

"Small disciplines repeated with consistency every day lead to great achievements gained slowly over time."

— John C Maxwell

Things to Accomplish

- _____
- _____
- _____
- _____
- _____
- _____
- _____

Action List

- _____
- _____
- _____
- _____
- _____
- _____
- _____

For Tomorrow

 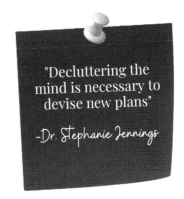

IDEAS

THOUGHTS

REMEMBER ME

DUMP IT

Notes

I decree and declare *greater* works and <u>greater</u> opportunities.

"Small disciplines repeated with consistency every day lead to great achievements gained slowly over time."

– John C Maxwell

Things to Accomplish

- _____
- _____
- _____
- _____
- _____
- _____
- _____
- _____

Action List

- _____
- _____
- _____
- _____
- _____
- _____
- _____

For Tomorrow

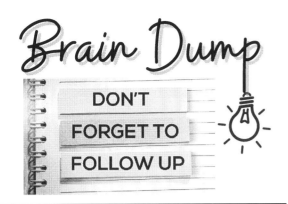

IDEAS

THOUGHTS

REMEMBER ME

DUMP IT

Notes

I decree and declare new joy and new *strenth*.

"Small disciplines repeated with consistency every day lead to great achievements gained slowly over time."

– John C Maxwell

Things to Accomplish

-
-
-
-
-
-
-

Action List

-
-
-
-
-
-
-

For Tomorrow

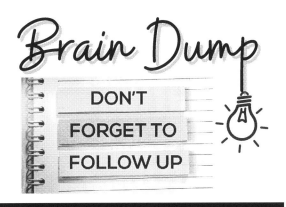

IDEAS

THOUGHTS

REMEMBER ME

DUMP IT

Notes

DEAR Monday

I decree and declare <u>NO MORE</u> dead ends or dead works in *Jesus* name.

"Small disciplines repeated with consistency every day lead to great achievements gained slowly over time."

- John C Maxwell

Things to Accomplish

-
-
-
-
-
-
-

Action List

-
-
-
-
-
-
-

For Tomorrow

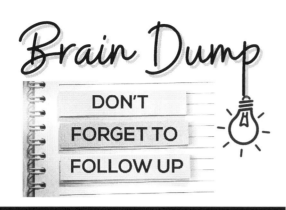

IDEAS

THOUGHTS

REMEMBER ME

DUMP IT

Notes

I decree and declare *possibilities* and new prosperity.

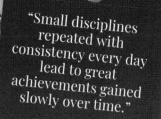

"Small disciplines repeated with consistency every day lead to great achievements gained slowly over time."

— John C Maxwell

Things to Accomplish

- _____
- _____
- _____
- _____
- _____
- _____
- _____

Action List

- _____
- _____
- _____
- _____
- _____
- _____
- _____

For Tomorrow

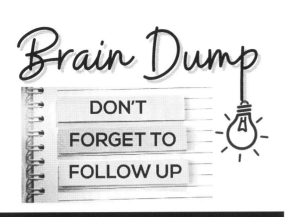
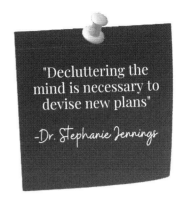

IDEAS

THOUGHTS

REMEMBER ME

DUMP IT

Notes

DEAR *monday*

I decree and declare I have the Spirit of a *conquer*.

"Small disciplines repeated with consistency every day lead to great achievements gained slowly over time."

– John C Maxwell

Things to Accomplish

- _____
- _____
- _____
- _____
- _____
- _____
- _____

Action List

- _____
- _____
- _____
- _____
- _____
- _____
- _____

For Tomorrow

 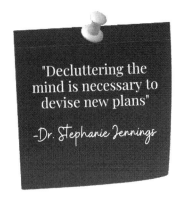

IDEAS

THOUGHTS

REMEMBER ME

DUMP IT

Notes

I decree and declare <u>multiplied</u> blessings.

"Small disciplines repeated with consistency every day lead to great achievements gained slowly over time."

– John C Maxwell

Things to Accomplish

- _____
- _____
- _____
- _____
- _____
- _____
- _____

Action List

- _____
- _____
- _____
- _____
- _____
- _____
- _____

For Tomorrow

IDEAS

THOUGHTS

REMEMBER ME

DUMP IT

Notes

I decree and declare new *adventures* and new <u>memories</u>.

"Small disciplines repeated with consistency every day lead to great achievements gained slowly over time."

– John C Maxwell

Things to Accomplish

- _____
- _____
- _____
- _____
- _____
- _____
- _____

Action List

- _____
- _____
- _____
- _____
- _____
- _____
- _____

For Tomorrow

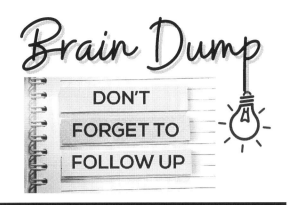

IDEAS

THOUGHTS

REMEMBER ME

DUMP IT

Notes

DEAR *Monday*

I decree and declare <u>all things</u> are *accomplished* and every assignment is *finished*.

"Small disciplines repeated with consistency every day lead to great achievements gained slowly over time."

– John C Maxwell

Things to Accomplish

-
-
-
-
-
-
-

Action List

-
-
-
-
-
-
-

For Tomorrow

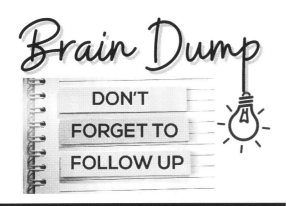 

IDEAS

THOUGHTS

REMEMBER ME

DUMP IT

Notes

DEAR *Monday*

I decree and declare double *miracles*, double *momentum* and double *manifestations*.

> "Small disciplines repeated with consistency every day lead to great achievements gained slowly over time."
>
> – John C Maxwell

Things to Accomplish

- _____
- _____
- _____
- _____
- _____
- _____
- _____

Action List

- _____
- _____
- _____
- _____
- _____
- _____
- _____

For Tomorrow

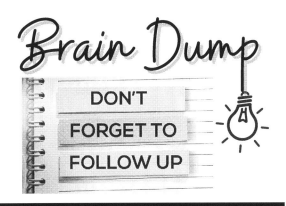
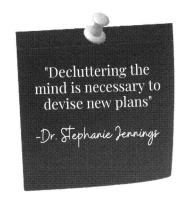

IDEAS

THOUGHTS

REMEMBER ME

DUMP IT

Notes

DEAR *Monday*

I decree and declare *bolder,* BIGGER, better.

"Small disciplines repeated with consistency every day lead to great achievements gained slowly over time."

– John C Maxwell

Things to Accomplish

-
-
-
-
-
-
-

Action List

-
-
-
-
-
-
-

For Tomorrow

 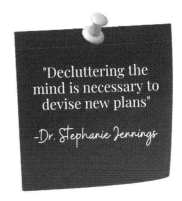

IDEAS

THOUGHTS

REMEMBER ME

DUMP IT

Notes

DEAR Monday

I <u>decree</u> and declare restoration, release, and *restitution*.

"Small disciplines repeated with consistency every day lead to great achievements gained slowly over time."

— John C Maxwell

Things to Accomplish

- ___
- ___
- ___
- ___
- ___
- ___
- ___

Action List

- ___
- ___
- ___
- ___
- ___
- ___
- ___

For Tomorrow

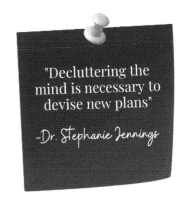

IDEAS

THOUGHTS

REMEMBER ME

DUMP IT

Notes

Notes

Notes

Notes

Notes

Notes

Notes

Notes

Notes

Notes

Notes

Notes

Notes

Notes

Notes

Notes

Notes

Notes

Notes

Notes

Notes

Notes

Notes

Notes

Notes

Notes

Notes

Notes

Notes

Notes

Made in United States
Orlando, FL
10 January 2023